# Why You Do This To Me

An Echo of Unsent Words

-da sachin sharma

Copyright © <2025> <da sachin sharma>

*It started with maybe. It ends with maybe.*
*This book lives in the space between.*

Dedication


*In loving memory of my father Poonam Chand Sharma,
whom I lost in the quiet beginning of January 2025,
and
for my dear friend Aashish, whom I was lucky enough to
find again after almost twenty years, only to have to say
goodbye when he left us in September 2024.*

*I had such a great time with both of you. The
conversations, the laughter, the connection... the most
amazing moments. In the quiet that follows, I find myself
wondering if this was just destiny. I have this thought...
maybe some people grace our lives with the most
incredible, most vibrant moments precisely because they
only have a short time to spend with us. Maybe the
beauty of their presence is so sharp, so intense, because
they have to leave us too soon.*

*Maybe.*

*Losing you both has left me standing in the same place,
haunted by the same quiet, aching question over and
over again—a question that is the very heart of every
page in this book:*

*Why did you leave me? Why did you do this to me?*

*This is for you.*

# Maybe

*It started with a maybe, soft and low, A hesitant and hopeful, tender glow. It ends with maybe, whispered to the night, Lost somewhere between the dark and light.*

*Maybe you've moved on now, strong and free, (A story that I tell myself, you see). Maybe you reach out, then you pull back your hand, Lost in a silence we both misunderstand?*

*Maybe these pages, holding thoughts run deep, Are just a way for memory to keep. Or maybe writing helps the heart let go, Of feelings I don't want the world to know.*

*Maybe the 'why' we never understood, Was never meant to be resolved for good. Maybe the questions burning in the air, Are burdens only solitude can bear.*

*Maybe we'll meet, when twenty years have flown, On some street corner, suddenly alone Together, finding words we couldn't say, And watch regrets like shadows melt away.*

*Or maybe 'us' is just a story told, Becoming faint, inevitably old. Fading like music from a distant car, Leaving behind a lonely, wishing star.*
*Maybe we live now, only in these lines, Reflected in the reader's searching signs. Or maybe dawn will bring a different view...*

*Maybe.*

# Acknowledgments

My deepest thanks go out to every single person who has walked into, or even just briefly brushed past, the path of my life. Each encounter, however small or significant, leaves a trace, sparks a thought, or becomes part of an unseen story that shapes who we are.

While the voice threading through these pages is undeniably mine, the feelings and experiences echoed here draw from more than just my own heart. They are fragments inspired by many lives I've observed, relationships I've witnessed or imagined, all woven together with my personal threads of memory, longing, and quiet reflection. In a way, this book holds pieces of many different hearts, beating with a similar, melancholic rhythm.

This collection isn't intended simply as an expression of sadness, though sadness is certainly present here. If anything, I hope it feels like a quiet exploration – maybe even a gentle celebration – of that peculiar, pervasive melancholic feeling that often resides somewhere deep within us. The feeling we are sometimes taught to ignore, to numb, or to run away from. Writing these thoughts down, giving them space, felt less like running away and more like turning around to finally face that feeling. Quietly. Honestly.

They say you never truly die, that you achieve a kind of immortality, if an artist loves you. Perhaps being an artist only in my own feelings and simple words, here I am, writing them all down – the people, the moments, the connections felt, the echoes that remain. This is my way of trying to keep them alive, remembered, breathing softly between these lines, granting them a small measure of that immortality.

To all my love – the ones that were real, tangible, undeniably present... and also to the ones that lived more vividly in my imagination, in my hopes, in my countless 'maybes'.

I am truly grateful to everyone who came into my life and touched me somewhere significant, leaving a mark, subtly changing my direction, teaching me something, or simply sharing a quiet moment that lingered.

And **you**... yes, **you**. The specific 'you' these thoughts so often circle back to, the quiet audience for these unsent words... **you** remain special. That feeling hasn't faded. Today, tomorrow, and forever... **you** hold that unique space.

Who knows... maybe after reading all these pages, feeling these echoes from my heart... maybe **you** will fall in love with me once again.

Or maybe not. It remains, like so much else between us perhaps... just another maybe.

# Introduction

*"Why you do this to me?"*

Sometimes, it feels less like a direct question aimed at someone specific, and more like a constant, low hum beneath the surface of everyday life. An ache. The kind that gets louder in the deep quiet of the night, when the city outside finally sleeps but your own mind refuses to rest, circling the same thoughts, the same memories, the same unanswered questions.

What you hold in your hands isn't a story in the way you might expect. This book won't give you clear answers, nor will it tell a story with a straightforward plot, a beginning, middle, and satisfying end. These are just... thoughts. Fragments. The kind that surface when you're staring at the ceiling at 3 AM, replaying moments like broken film reels. The kind you type out carefully into the cold glow of a phone screen, read back once, twice, maybe hover over 'send', and then delete with a heavy sigh because the words feel too raw, too vulnerable, or maybe just... useless to dispatch into an echoing silence.

It's a collection built on the shifting sands of 'what if' and 'if only'. It breathes the air of 'maybe'. Maybe you felt that initial connection in the canteen just as strongly as I did. Maybe the reasons I've invented in my head for your silence are gentler, more bearable, than the actual truth might be. Maybe, sometimes, you also pick up your phone, your thumb hovering over my name, before pulling back just like I do. Maybe those little routines we shared – the morning songs never shared now, the late-night talks ending in imagined hugs – maybe they held a quiet importance for you too. Maybe you still have those silly folded-paper origami roses tucked away somewhere safe, perhaps pressed inside "The Silent Patient." Maybe not.

These pages are a collection of those unsent messages, those internal monologues, those quiet reflections and persistent questions often addressed to a 'you' who isn't listening, or perhaps can't listen anymore, or maybe simply chose to stop. It's about the confusing, painful journey from a hopeful 'maybe' to an abrupt 'not allowed' and the lingering emptiness of 'nothing'. It's about missing someone so much that even a Mumbai traffic jam could feel like a precious gift, simply because it bought a few more minutes together. It's about loving reasonlessly, not being able to hate, and wondering if you were easily replaceable. It's in the muscle memory that folds a paper rose from a straw wrapper, a fragile echo later abandoned on a cafe table.

This is the sound of connection lost, of words trapped behind a suddenly reappeared poker face, of a heart trying to navigate the vast, quiet space left behind. It's melancholic, it's simple, it's honest. It's the feeling of standing still while the world rushes past.

Maybe reading these thoughts feels like listening in on someone else's quiet, internal monologue late at night. Maybe, just maybe, you'll find your own echoes reflected here too.

Maybe.

It's late again. Way past midnight here in Mumbai. The city outside my window is finally starting to quiet down, breathing a little easier in the deep darkness. Inside my head, though... it's loud. Crowded. Full of words I can't bring myself to send you. Full of feelings that seem to have nowhere else to go but circle endlessly within me.

My thumb often hovers over the keypad... sometimes over the empty space where your name *used* to be listed in my phone contacts. Deleted now, of course. A futile attempt to create distance, maybe? A way to stop the impulse? But the number... like you... isn't really forgotten. Never truly forgotten.

What would I even type if I let myself? Just a simple 'Hey'? Or maybe the honest truth: 'Thinking of you'? Or perhaps the question that always bubbles up, raw and unanswered: 'Why?'

Each potential message feels heavy... and ultimately pointless before it's even written. Like whispering your deepest secrets into a hurricane... expecting some kind of answer back, but knowing deep down there will only be silence. If I did press send, the 'delivered' receipt probably wouldn't even appear. Just... *sent*. Dispatched into the digital void where you seem to exist now... a place my messages can't reach anymore. Or maybe, more painfully, a place you just choose not to answer from.

So, I close the keypad. Lock the phone screen, making it go dark again. Turn away from the potential connection. Stare into the actual darkness of my quiet room. And I'm left alone once more, with all the unspoken words trapped inside my chest, heavy and restless.

This book... these pages... maybe this is where those unsent messages finally get to live. A place for them to breathe. Maybe putting them down here, giving them form, makes them feel a little more real. Gives them somewhere to exist, even if they never, ever reach your eyes.

Maybe.

# Why You Do This To Me

My thumb hovers over your name. Again. Just to type 'Hey'. But what's the point? It probably won't even say 'delivered'. Just... sent. Sent into nothing. Like my feelings. Why did you make 'nothing' the place where my feelings go?

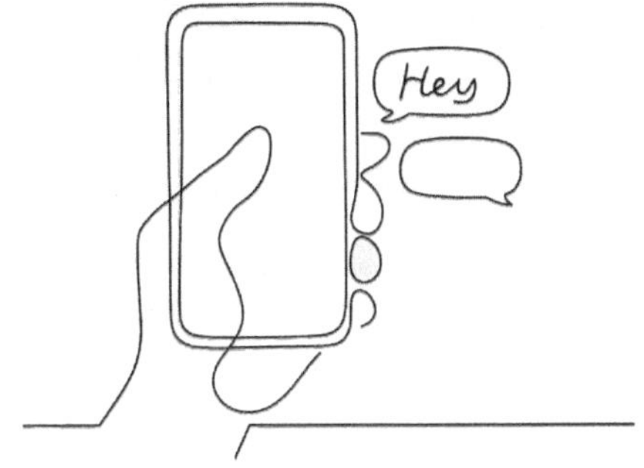

I saw something today that made me laugh, just like you used to. For a second, I reached for my phone to tell you all about it... then I remembered. The line is cut. The door is closed. Why do you still live so loudly in my memory when you're so silent in my life?

# Why You Do This To Me

Remember how you loved that silly song? It came on the radio today. My heart did that little flip... that 'wooo...' thing it does when I think of you. But this time, it wasn't happy. It was just... remembering. Like a phantom limb aching for something that isn't there. Why does the music still play when our conversation stopped?

I trace the outline of your smile in my mind. The way it crinkled your eyes. I wonder if you still smile like that. I hope you do. But a part of me aches, wishing I could be the reason, just one more time. Why did you take your smile away from my world?

# Why You Do This To Me

They say 'block and delete' makes it easier. Maybe for you. But for me? You're not deleted. You're here, in my head, in the spaces between my breaths. Blocking a number doesn't block a heart, does it? Why do you get to switch off your feelings, while mine are stuck on 'on'?

I wrote you another message tonight. Long. Full of everything I can't say. Then I deleted it, letter by letter. It felt like erasing myself, just a little bit. Because if my words can't reach you, do they even exist? Why do you make me doubt my own voice?

# Why You Do This To Me

Sometimes I imagine you accidentally unblocking me. Maybe you'd see the string of 'missed calls' or unsent 'thinking of you's. Would you feel anything? Or would you just block me again, faster this time? Why does wondering about your reaction hurt almost as much as the silence?

I was walking past the station yesterday evening... just heading somewhere else... and I saw the bakery. You know the one. *Our* bakery, I always thought of it in my head. The place we used to duck into all the time for those specific pastries you liked... or just some munchies... sometimes just to sit for a bit away from the rush.

It looked... wrong. Quiet. The usual bright sign was off. Shutters pulled down tight, looking dusty already. And a sad, slightly faded sign taped crookedly to the glass just said 'Permanently Closed'.

I clearly remember it opening... seemed like it was brand new right around the same time we first properly met and started spending time together. It feels like its story somehow started right alongside ours.

And now... seeing it shut down like that... it feels strangely like its story ended too, not so long after ours did. I wonder... probably a silly thought, getting sentimental about a shop... but was its lifespan somehow tied to ours? Did it close down because its best characters stopped visiting?

Was the bakery missing you, I wonder? Missing *us*... sitting at that little table we usually tried to get near the window... sharing pastries... talking for hours... laughing about something stupid? Maybe.

Seeing it gone for good... it makes this whole street feel different now when I walk down it alone. Definitely emptier. It's not just the familiar emptiness of you not being here beside me... but now there's the added emptiness of *our place* being gone too. A double void on a once-familiar road. It just feels... sadder.

It's Thursday afternoon, and I'm sitting here at Starbucks... the usual buzz of chatter and coffee machines all around me. My hand is wrapped around a warm cup, but it still feels... incomplete somehow. It made me think of yours.

Your hands... I remember them so clearly. So beautiful. I remember the way your long, sleek fingers looked... I always found them so elegant. They were soft to the touch, yet I also remember thinking they were so strong. That contrast... delicate beauty and quiet strength all in one... it was so uniquely *you*.

My favorite place for my hand was inside yours. It just... fit. Perfectly. Like a key finally finding its own specific lock. The way your long fingers would curl around mine... it was a feeling of complete safety, of being anchored.

I have this little personal theory... a belief, maybe... that people with long fingers like yours think a lot. Really think things through. That they turn over every detail, every possibility, looking at a problem from every angle before making any important decision.

And now, sitting here... that thought hurts in a new way. Because if my silly theory is even a little bit true... it means you thought about it. A lot. The decision to let go... it wasn't just a sudden impulse or a fleeting moment of anger. It must have been a conclusion you reached after a long, quiet, internal debate with yourself. You must have weighed it all, carefully.

# Why You Do This To Me

Remembering that... and feeling this cold emptiness now, even in a crowded cafe... it makes the final question feel even heavier, more impossible to understand.

After all that thinking... all that careful consideration... why did you still let go? Why did you decide that was the right answer?

It was evening, just as the sun was setting, walking near the controlled chaos of the station. That time of day when everyone is rushing to get home, a river of tired faces and hurried footsteps flowing all around. And amidst all that human motion, I saw him. The funniest little brown street dog, spinning in frantic, happy circles on the pavement, absolutely determined to catch his own tail as if it were the most important mission in the world.

He was so focused, so comically serious about his impossible task. And it was exactly the kind of silly, simple, everyday magic we used to always point out to each other. I could almost hear your voice in my head, a gentle elbow nudge, a whispered, "Look at that." I could almost hear your specific laugh... the one you had for things just like this.

My hand went to my pocket and pulled out my phone... completely on autopilot. A reflex built over a long time, I guess. I opened the camera app, even zoomed in a little to frame the perfect shot of the dizzying little dog, ready to capture the moment. My first, immediate thought was, *You have to see this, this is hilarious.*

But then... my thumb just stopped. Hovering over the button to take the picture. The thought I was sending it *to*... the person I was capturing it *for*... it suddenly hit a dead end.

Who was I actually taking this picture for? Who would I send it to, expecting an immediate "Haha, what an idiot" text back? The recipient for that kind of shared, silly, pointless joy... your name... it isn't there anymore.

# Why You Do This To Me

The impulse to share my world with you, even the smallest, most random parts of it... it's still so strong, so deeply ingrained. And the crash of remembering, every single time, that I can't... it's breathtaking in its own quiet, painful way.

I just... slowly, quietly, put my phone back into my pocket without taking the picture. The funny little dog kept spinning on the pavement, completely oblivious. But he didn't feel funny to me anymore. His happy, solitary game just made me feel... deeply, profoundly lonely right there in the middle of the crowd.

Here at Bandstand... my favourite place in all of Mumbai, but tonight it feels different. More chaotic, yet lonelier. Down on the promenade, a man is sitting on the edge, playing a guitar and singing some sad, soulful song. A small crowd has gathered around him, their faces illuminated by phone screens, lost in his music. And behind it all, the Arabian Sea is restless, grey, and choppy, smashing against the rocks like it has an argument it can't win.

My eyes wander from the singer... past the quiet crowd... towards the dark crevices of the rocks further down. It's the usual sight. Young couples tucked away in the shadows, trying to steal a private moment in a very public place. A sad smile almost touches my lips... because I remember. I remember how **we** used to sit on these very stairs... and watch them... and quietly laugh together, making up stories about their over-the-top PDA. We judged them a little, didn't we?

Because we never needed all of that. Our intimacy was different. Quieter. **We** could sit here for an hour... on these same cold stone stairs... without saying a single word to each other. Just watching the sea, feeling the breeze, comfortable... connected. A whole silent conversation happening between us that no one else could ever hear. That was *our* kind of closeness.

And looking at the sea now... its relentless, angry crashing... a new thought forms in my head. It's not just matching my mood tonight. No. It feels like the sea itself is missing **you**. Like it's restless *because* **you**'re not here to sit and watch it. Like it's crashing against the rocks in frustration, searching for the other person who used to appreciate its quiet, steady company.

So I just stand here, a lonely observer caught between a sad song I don't know and a restless sea that feels as heartbroken as I do. Tonight, it seems... even the ocean misses **you**.

Watching a film this afternoon... just trying to switch off my brain for a couple of hours. And then this one shot... a particular scene... it just hit me out of nowhere. Like a flashback. Took me right back, years ago maybe... all the way back to our very first kiss.

Do you remember it? How it felt like we were stealing a moment? Like snatching something precious that wasn't quite ours to take, not yet anyway. It was so quick. It probably lasted just for a few seconds... maybe not even one full second, looking back now, it seemed to happen so fast. But inside my head, in my memory... that tiny moment stretches out... sometimes it feels like it lasted forever. And it instantly, immediately left me wanting more.

That tiny, stolen moment... honestly, thinking about it now, maybe it *was* the best moment of my life up until that point. It felt that significant, that intense.

And then what happened right after? Do you remember that too? That sudden, heavy, awkward silence settling between us like dust. That feeling of numbness... maybe both of us blushing... completely unsure of everything. Looking at each other... maybe quickly looking away... neither of us having any idea what to do next. Should we lean in again? Should we just try to laugh it off? Should we just turn around and quickly leave? That uncertainty...

Remembering that whole sequence... the intense, stolen kiss and the clumsy, numb confusion right after... it's all so incredibly vivid today, sparked by a random

# Why You Do This To Me

scene in a movie. Funny how memory works like that. Or maybe just... painful. Yeah. Probably just painful.

Friday night at the mall... lots of people moving around. So many lights. Then I smelled it. That smell... your smell. You always smelled like that. I just stopped walking. Right there. People bumped into me. I didn't care. For just a second, I thought... you are here. Really here. I looked around fast. My heart was beating hard. Hoping... really hoping it was you. But no. It was just some lady walking away. The smell was gone. And I felt... empty then. Like I missed a step going down the stairs. Like I reached out my hand for you... and there was just air. Nothing.

# Why You Do This To Me

Thinking about Mumbai rains today... not because it's raining now, but because a memory surfaced. That specific evening it was pouring down, absolutely relentless. You called me... completely stranded near the station, maybe? No rickshaw, no cab stopping for you in that downpour.

Then I spotted you under a shop awning... soaked through. Your white t-shirt was clinging to you, your hair plastered to your face, and I remember watching you try to push wet strands out of your eyes while looking around, clearly irritated with the whole situation... but somehow, even then, looking incredibly beautiful.

You saw me pull up, raised your hand in a quick 'Hi', maybe a little surprised. I think I just stared for a second... probably completely zoned out, just taking in the sight of you standing there in the rain. You just seemed relieved, said "Thank God," and climbed onto the back of my bike without hesitation. That was the first time you'd ever ridden on it with me.

I remember feeling you shivering slightly behind me from the cold wind and the rain as we rode through the wet, slick streets. When we finally reached your place, you quickly hopped off, turned, gave me that sudden, bright smile – the kind that lit up everything despite the grey weather – said a quick 'Bye!', and dashed inside out of the rain.

No 'thank you' for the ride. I remember registering that clearly. And I remember thinking in that exact moment...

*okay, this is good. This means something.* It meant, in my mind then, that we were close enough now... comfortable enough... that we didn't need those polite, formal words between us anymore for simple favors. Maybe we really were that close then. Or maybe I just desperately wanted to believe we were, reading meaning into the missing words.

But that final smile... the 'Bye' one... *that* felt undeniably real. Genuine. That specific smile, caught in the rain... it's still so vivid in my memory. Feels like it's stored away somewhere safe and warm, deep inside my heart. A tiny, bright light that remains from that cold, wet day.

## Why You Do This To Me

Got good news today. An email. About my work project... the one I worked on for so long. So many late nights. It's approved now. Finished. I felt so happy... like something heavy lifted off.

I wanted to tell someone right away. My hand just picked up my phone. My fingers started typing your name... without me even thinking. Like they always did. I could almost hear your voice in my head... getting excited for me... asking lots of questions. You always did that. But then... I stopped. My thumb just froze over the screen. Who am I sending this to? The happy feeling... it just disappeared. Gone.

The room felt so quiet then. Too quiet. Your happy voice should be here. But it's just... silent. The good news... it feels a little less good now. Being alone with it.

Looking in my desk drawer today... trying to find batteries. My fingers found something else instead. That little robot keychain. Remember it? You bought it for me at that market. It had a funny serious face... and a wobbly head. I forgot it was even in there. I just sat and held it for a minute. The metal felt cool. Then it got warm in my hand.

I remembered you laughing when you gave it to me... saying I look serious like the little robot when I think hard. It's such a small thing. Really small. But holding it... it felt heavy. So heavy. Full of memories... of us.

What do you do with things like this? Things that remind you? I just put it back in the drawer. Pushed it way to the back. Into the dark. It felt strange. Like hiding something important... because looking at it hurts too much right now.

# Why You Do This To Me

Remember your fingers? How I always used to play with them whenever we met? When we were sitting close... maybe talking... my hand would just find yours.

And I'd press your knuckles... remember? Gently... just being playful.

Your smile would vanish. Like *poof.* Gone.

And then that look would come on your face... so irritated. You'd try to pull your hand away... sometimes you'd huff a little.

Even the very first time we met... I did it. I saw that first smile change... right away... into your 'stop doing that' face.

Funny... the things you remember. Now... I really miss seeing that irritated look. I miss your hand being there... close enough for me to annoy. Just... miss it being there at all.

Had to rush into Starbucks for a work meeting earlier today... grabbed my usual order just to keep me going – Java Chip Frappuccino, extra shot. Got the drink, found a table, the meeting started, hashing out details for some project.

We were right in the middle of discussing something important... when the guy I was meeting paused, looked down towards my hands, and said, "Wow, that looks like a rose." And I glanced down... and realized I'd done it again. Without even consciously thinking about it, my restless fingers had twisted and folded the paper straw cover into a tiny, intricate rose. Pure muscle memory. Pure habit.

Just like I used to do *all the time* whenever we met, remember? Sitting across from each other in a cafe, maybe waiting for food, maybe just talking... my hands would always find something – a tissue, a straw cover, a napkin corner – and fold it into some little shape while we talked. A bird, a plane, a ring, often a rose. And you... you always used to carefully take them when I was done. Sometimes you'd smile. Sometimes you'd just tuck them carefully into your pocket or bag, like they were actually something precious, not just folded paper.

Do you still have any of them? That little, fragile collection of folded paper things? Maybe? Or maybe not? I sometimes picture one tucked away safely as a forgotten

# Why You Do This To Me

bookmark... maybe even pressed flat between the pages of that copy of "The Silent Patient" you were reading when we first met in that other cafe? Or maybe... maybe they just got lost over time... swept away inadvertently, like other small things were. Like we were.

After the meeting finished today... I looked at the little paper rose sitting there on the table beside my empty Frappuccino cup. And I just... left it behind. Didn't pick it up to put in my own pocket. It didn't feel right, somehow. Didn't feel like mine to keep anymore.

Out with friends tonight... just talking, trying to relax. It's Friday evening. Then a phone screen lit up on the table nearby. My friend's phone.

And your name flashed on it. Big and clear.

Just for that split second... my heart did that stupid jump. That lurch it does. My brain went fuzzy... thinking... Is that my phone? Is that... for me? From you?

Hope is such a quick reflex, isn't it? Even now.

Then... reality. No. Of course not. Wrong phone. Your call... or your message... it was for them. Not for me.

Seeing your name appear so easily like that... so normally... on someone else's screen... while my own screen stays so quiet from you...

It's a strange, sharp kind of ache. Feels like watching you wave hello... but to the person standing right behind me.

# Why You Do This To Me

It's late now... quiet Friday night here. Thinking...

Why did you say goodbye?

Was it one big reason? Something I missed? Or was it lots of little things... piling up silently over time?

Did you plan it out? Know that day was the day you'd say it? Or did the moment just... arrive? Did the words just happen?

Did you feel sad when it happened... or maybe just... relieved? Free?

I go over it again and again in my head sometimes. The ending. Whether it was an actual word you said, or just... the silence that screamed goodbye all on its own.

Just trying to understand the 'why'. The reason behind your goodbye. Maybe there isn't one clear answer. Maybe that's the hardest part. The not knowing for sure... it still aches. Deep down.

My heart still does that sometimes... even after all this time. That stupid little 'wooo...' jump inside my chest. It happens when a random memory of you just ambushes me... maybe triggered by a song, a smell, nothing at all. It's like an echo of that old excitement I used to feel just thinking about you. Back then, it made me smile... made me want to reach out... text you something flirty or sweet.

But now? The feeling just... flickers for a second and fades away so fast. It leaves behind this quiet stillness. And a heavy, hollow feeling right in the center of my chest... where all that warmth used to spread from. No words come to mind anymore.

Just... silence. And the memory of a feeling I can't seem to fully grasp again.

# Why You Do This To Me

It's so quiet now... the deep part of the night. Even the city sounds are muted. And right now, I can picture your smile so clearly in my head. It's like a photograph imprinted behind my eyes.

That specific little curve of your lips... the way your eyes would crinkle slightly at the corners when it was real. Back then, seeing you smile felt like the sun coming out after rain. It made everything feel okay, somehow lighter. Now, remembering it alone in the dark... it just makes the quiet in this room feel heavier, deeper.

Why does a memory that holds so much past happiness feel so sad to hold onto now? It's like looking at a beautiful picture of someone you loved... someone you can't ever speak to again.

Your eyes... yeah, my thoughts drift back to them again. How they could change so quickly, like the sea. One moment sparkling with mischief... a silent joke passing between us.

The next, they'd be so deep and thoughtful... like you were seeing something far off that I couldn't grasp. Mysterious. I used to get lost just looking into them... trying to understand what was really going on inside your head, inside your heart. Trying to read the signs.

Now I just wonder... did you ever really see me? The actual, complicated, messy me underneath everything? Or was I just looking at a beautiful, reflective surface... seeing the feelings I wanted to believe were there?

# Why You Do This To Me

It still happens more often than I'd like to admit. Sometimes I just... zone out completely. Could be walking down a busy street, surrounded by noise and people... could be sitting right here, staring at the patterns on the wall. My mind just slips the leash... goes straight back into thinking about you. Replaying conversations, remembering moments. Totally lost for a minute or two.

It used to be a pleasant escape... a happy daydream bubble. Now it feels... different. More like getting lost in a thick fog, unable to see the way forward. Or wandering through the rooms of an empty house that still echoes with old laughter... knowing it's just ghosts now. And snapping back to the present reality feels... jarring. Like waking up suddenly to a cold room.

My hand feels cold tonight. Lying here on the sheets, empty. But it remembers holding yours. Muscle memory is strange like that. It remembers the shape... the comfortable weight... the warmth. How easily your fingers used to link with mine when we walked. Like they were made to fit together.

That simple feeling of connection... just walking side-by-side, hands joined, not needing words. It felt solid. Easy. Grounding. Safe. Now... it's just my own empty palm against the cool fabric.

Remembering that feeling of holding your hand... it doesn't bring comfort. It just makes the emptiness right here, right now, feel sharper, more defined. Like knowing exactly what's missing and knowing it's not coming back.

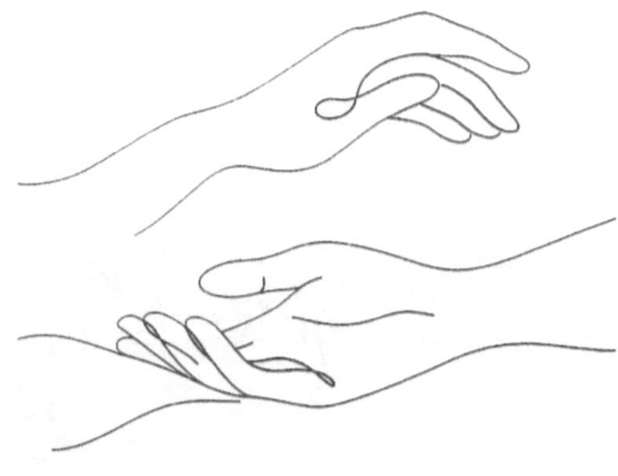

# Why You Do This To Me

Thinking about being close enough to you... resting my head near yours... close enough to watch the corner of your lip twitch just before you smiled. Imagining leaning in... just a fraction... a soft kiss right there. Feeling the smile start against my own lips. That was such a sweet, private daydream once. A quiet, hopeful thought I held onto tightly.

Remembering that fantasy now... thinking about that specific, imagined closeness... it feels almost cruel. Like my own mind betraying me with memories of intimacy that never fully happened, or that can't happen again. That simple touch... that connection I craved so deeply... it feels like it belongs to another universe now. A million light-years away.

A beautiful, painful dream from a past life that has absolutely no connection to this empty room and this lonely early morning.

Piano music... drifting in softly from somewhere outside. Or maybe it's just playing low on someone's radio nearby. It's so quiet now... early Monday morning.

When I hear piano now... any piano tune at all... my first thought, every single time... it goes straight to you.

Is that your tune? The one you were always working on... humming the notes... trying to get that one part just right? Remember?

My ears perk up automatically. I find myself listening closely... trying to catch the specific melody through the distance or the quiet static. Wondering... is that you playing? Did you ever finish it?

It's a silly thought, I know it is. Logically. It's never you. Never that specific tune you were making.

But for just a moment... my heart does a little hopeful pause. Because the sound of piano keys now... any piano... it just feels connected to the memory of you. Like your soundtrack is still playing somewhere out there.

# Why You Do This To Me

Why do we run away? It's past 12:30 AM... the city outside is mostly quiet now. A good time for these kinds of heavy thoughts.

People run from difficult situations... from tough conversations... sometimes even from people they once felt close to. Why is that the first instinct sometimes? Is it just... fear?

Did you run away? From me... or was it from something harder... something inside yourself you couldn't face?

It's strange... sometimes people seem to run away even from good things. From laughter... from a chance at happiness... maybe afraid it won't last, or maybe feeling like they don't deserve it. And they run from tears too... terrified of falling apart if they let the sadness show.

It's confusing... this human habit of escape. Building walls instead of figuring things out.

Did running away make it easier for you, I wonder? Does avoiding the difficult stuff ever really make it better in the end? Or does it just leave everything... broken? Unfinished? Hanging in the silence forever?

Leaving the people left behind just wondering... why. Always... why.

Went to Starbucks earlier. Was about to order my usual black coffee... same as always. But didn't. Instead, I just pointed to the top of the menu board. The first drink listed. The person taking the order looked a bit surprised. Honestly, I was surprised too. Why did I even do that?

The drink came... it was cold, sweetish. Definitely not my usual taste. Then it clicked. **You** used to do that sometimes. Ordering random things... **you** called it a 'taste adventure' or something. Did my brain just copy **you**?

Sitting there alone, drinking that strange drink... it felt empty. Like an echo of **you** and **your** habit, but without **you** actually being there.

Just a weird reminder of a little thing I picked up... from someone who isn't here anymore.

# Why You Do This To Me

It's strange how it works... especially now, in the quiet of the early morning when my mind drifts so easily.

Sometimes, when I really get lost in my thoughts... deep down inside my head... replaying moments we shared... imagining conversations we might have had...

In those times, lost in the memories... it feels like you're close again. Almost real. Like I could almost reach out and you'd be there. The sharp ache of missing you... it seems to soften for a little while then. It feels... comforting, almost.

But then... something always pulls me back. A noise outside... the clock ticking... just realizing where I am. Back to reality. Back to this quiet room... the empty space beside me.

And bam. The missing feeling hits again. But it feels different. Sharper, somehow. More intense than before I drifted off into the memory.

So... is it good? Is it helpful? Getting lost in those thoughts? Finding that temporary feeling of closeness? Or does it just make waking up to the reality... the hard fact that you're *not* here... hurt even more every single time?

I really don't know if it's good or bad anymore. I just know it happens.

That wave hits sometimes... often comes out of nowhere in the quiet. Like right now, in this stillness.

The intense wave of missing you. So strong it feels like a physical need... like I absolutely *have* to see your face... hear your voice... right this very minute.

But I know I can't. The world outside... it won't just give you back to me.

So, what I've started doing now is... I just lower my head. Tilt it down, maybe close my eyes for a second. Take a slow breath. And I look inwards. Search inside my own chest... inside my heart.

And yes... there you are. Always. Like clockwork. A clear picture... a warm feeling... settled deep right there.

It's a quiet, maybe even sad kind of comfort... knowing the main place you live now is inside me, instead of out here walking beside me. But you *are* there. Found again. Every single time I look down and search for you.

# Why You Do This To Me

It's late... past 12:30 AM now. Thinking about love... and what people say about it. They try to put rules on it, don't they? Say you only truly fall in love once... maybe twice in your whole life if things get complicated.

My story feels different, though. It wasn't just a one-time fall with you. It feels... continuous. Like something that's still happening, even now.

Every time a clear thought of you comes into my head – and they visit often, especially in the quiet like this – it's like experiencing that feeling all over again. That same warmth spreading through my chest... that same undeniable pull towards you. It never really switched off.

Maybe 'falling' isn't the right word for what happens now. Maybe it's just... *being*. Being in love with you. Constantly. Day after day. Even when that love mostly lives inside my own heart now... tangled up with memories and this quiet, persistent ache. It just... is. A constant presence.

It sounds stupid, I know... sitting here trying to *make* myself hate you. But sometimes, late at night like this... when the missing feels particularly heavy... I think maybe hate would be easier. Maybe it would hurt less than this constant ache.

So I try. I really do. I sit here in the quiet and pull up the memories of the worst moments between us. The arguments. The misunderstandings. The times things felt really broken or unfair. I try to focus hard on the anger... the disappointment... the hurt feelings. Try to hold onto them tight, let them build into something solid.

But then... something else always happens. Without fail. Another memory sneaks in, uninvited. A different one. The way you laughed that one time, maybe. Or a quiet, comfortable silence we shared. Or just the simple feeling of being near you.

And just like that... poof. The anger I was trying so hard to build... it just dissolves. Like smoke drifting away. And I'm left just... feeling again. Remembering something good, something warm. Sometimes almost smiling at the memory before I catch myself. And feeling that familiar, stubborn wave of love wash over me again.

How does every memory, even the bad ones, somehow circle back to loving you? It makes no logical sense. But it's true. I've tried. And I've failed. I can't hate you. Not even a little tiny bit. It just isn't in me.

# Why You Do This To Me

It's that quiet time now... past midnight, the city breathing softly before the real morning rush begins. And in this stillness, I miss them. Those simple messages.

Your 'Good morning'... It used to arrive like the very first ray of sun touching the window... sometimes even before the actual dawn lit up the sky. A little digital piece of warmth to start the day.

And your 'Good night'... that felt like the day sighing softly... tucking itself in gently. The final, quiet word before drifting off to sleep.

Now... the sun still climbs into the sky each morning, of course. But the day doesn't *feel* like it begins the same way. That little spark... that first gentle hello... it's missing.

And the night... it doesn't get tucked in anymore. It just... falls. Deep into silence. Without that last soft word from you to close it.

Mornings and nights... they just aren't the same without your words marking the edges of the light and the dark. They feel... less held. Less bright. Just... different. Emptier somehow.

One second. Can a kiss even really happen in just one second? Ours did.

It was so fast. Stolen, really. Hurried. Maybe barely even there, if anyone else had been watching. But it was enough. Enough to feel... *something* electric. Enough to start this... this echo. This endless craving inside me.

It replays in my head sometimes... especially late at night like this... when everything outside is quiet and thoughts get loud. That single second. Playing over and over. And always followed by the feeling that comes right after it... wanting more. So much more.

Wanting a real kiss. A proper one. Long... slow... without the need to steal the moment... without looking over your shoulder.

But even now... thinking back... maybe I'd take anything. Even just... one more of those fleeting, stolen, one-second moments again. If only I could steal back time itself... just for that single second.

# Why You Do This To Me

Thinking about your fingers... remembering how they looked. Long... sleek... thoughtful somehow. I remember watching you drum them restlessly on tables when you were thinking hard about something. Or seeing you trace patterns on a misty windowpane... lost in thought.

Just watching your hands move while you talked or listened. It seems like such a small, insignificant detail... maybe silly to focus on it so much.

But why do these tiny little memories sometimes hurt the most? Like unexpected paper cuts throughout the day. Tiny sharp reminders popping up when I least expect them... catching me completely off guard. Leaving a small, stinging ache behind long after the memory fades.

You used to talk so much sometimes... Just blabbering away like a running stream. About your day at work... about some funny thing you saw on the train... about some random idea or theory... about total nonsense half the time. Just thinking out loud, filling the space.

I probably pretended to be only half-listening sometimes... maybe rolled my eyes playfully when you went off on a tangent. But secretly? I loved every word. The sound of your voice just filling the air around us... making ordinary moments feel alive, connected.

Now... the silence in my room is deafening. It presses in on me. I find myself straining sometimes, almost trying to hear it again. I'd give almost anything just to hear that stream of consciousness again... that familiar, unique blabber.

Even if it wasn't meant for me anymore. Just to have your voice break this silence.

# Why You Do This To Me

I clearly remember listening to you talk sometimes... maybe telling a story you were passionate about, or explaining something complicated... and getting completely lost. Not because I wasn't interested in the words... but because I was caught in a dilemma.

Half of me trying desperately to follow the thread of your conversation, trying to understand. The other half just wanting to ignore the words... wanting to just look into your eyes... trying to see past the surface, past the performance. Trying to dive deep... swim down and reach your heart somehow. I wanted so desperately to know... did your heart feel any of the same turbulent things mine did for you? Was there even a faint echo in there? Or was I just shouting my feelings into an empty, beautiful well?

That constant question... it still hovers in the back of my mind, especially late at night like this... Did your heart feel the same? Does it feel anything now?

It used to be a question filled with nervous hope. Tinged with excitement... anticipation... possibility. It was full of maybe's and what if's that I could build dreams on. Now... the question just hangs there in the quiet of the early morning. Heavy. Pointless. Unanswered. And maybe the silence *is* the answer.

Maybe the complete lack of any sign... any word... any gesture... is the sign itself. The clear, unspoken reply I never wanted to receive. And maybe accepting that silence for what it is... maybe that's the hardest part of trying to move on from this ache.

*Once felt, now empty?*

# Why You Do This To Me

You asked me once... or maybe it's just a question I imagine you asking in the silence... why did I ever love you? Why do I *still* feel this way now? It's late... past 1:45 AM... my mind is wide awake, turning this over.

And I think... it's not about how you look. Because beauty isn't forever, is it? It changes, it fades. That can't be the whole reason.

It's not just your smile... even though I loved your smile so much... because nobody can smile all the time. Life brings sadness too, moments when smiles are impossible. So that can't be it either.

And it can't be just our conversations... the way we used to talk... because they are silent now. You're not here. The talks have stopped. And yet... this feeling inside me hasn't stopped. It's still here. Solid. Unshaken.

So maybe... maybe there *is* no 'because'. No neat list of reasons I can tick off. Because if love only exists *because* of certain reasons... then it must die when those reasons change or disappear, right? If the reason is gone, the love should be gone too.

But mine isn't gone.

So maybe my love for you... it's just... a feeling. A deep connection that was formed that doesn't need a specific reason to keep existing. And maybe that's why it doesn't seem to know how to go away, even when logic says maybe it should.

I loved you without a list of reasons then. And I love you without needing reasons now. It just... is.

# Why You Do This To Me

It's late now... nearly 1 AM. Thinking about words... and the labels people put on them.

People talk about 'being romantic'. And they talk about 'being a flirt'. Like they are two totally separate roads you can choose to walk down.

But how I felt with you... the things I used to say... it didn't feel like I was on either of those roads. It felt like... maybe a third path? Something else entirely. Unnamed.

It wasn't calculated flirting, trying to score points or play a game. And it wasn't grand, sweeping romance copied from movies or poems. It was just... me. Whatever was inside my head or heart at that moment... spilling out. Sometimes it was funny, sometimes serious, sometimes maybe a little too intense or strange. Just... honest. unfiltered.

Maybe you heard 'poet' sometimes in my words. Maybe you heard 'flirt' other times. Maybe you heard 'romantic'. I don't really know what label you put on it all, if any.

What I *hoped* you heard? Was simply... me. My real voice. Sharing my real feelings as they came. For you.

I still don't have a proper name for that way of being... that 'third thing'. I only know that it felt real and true to me. And I miss having someone I could be that way with. I miss being that version of 'me' with you.

Thinking about relationships... the ones we choose to build, not the ones we're born into. Family is different.

But the other connections... based on love, or care, or just that spark... why do we feel this need to put a name on them? A specific tag... like 'friend', 'partner', 'lover', maybe even 'married'?

It feels like as soon as you stick that label on the connection... a rule book just appears out of nowhere. Suddenly there are expectations... unspoken rules... about how you're supposed to act now, what you're supposed to feel or not feel... all because of that name you've given it.

And wasn't it better before all that? Right at the beginning... when things were just... happening? Unfolding naturally? No labels needed. No rule book to follow, telling you how to be.

Just... two people. You being you. Me being me. Existing together in whatever way felt right. Sharing those feelings that didn't have a name... maybe they felt *more* real and honest *because* they didn't need a label attached.

Maybe the pressure to name it, to define it... maybe that's when we start losing the best part. That easy, unnamed beginning. That freedom. I miss that feeling sometimes. That simple, undefined 'us'.

# Why You Do This To Me

Now... 1 AM is the time the loneliness really sinks its teeth in deep. It's the time the missing you becomes a physical ache right in the center of my chest. The time the emptiness of this quiet room feels vast... echoing.

But it wasn't always like this, was it? This exact hour... 1 AM... it used to be *ours*.

Our special time. Just you and me. The noise and the endless rush of the city world outside would finally quiet down... seem to fade away... and it was just us. Maybe talking softly, maybe just sitting in comfortable silence. Connected. Safe. Away from all the chaos.

Now... the hour is still quiet. But the connection is gone. The safety is gone. And *our* time... somehow it got twisted around... turned into my loneliest hour. How does the best time turn into the hardest time? It feels so unfair.

It's quiet again... thinking about beginnings. How things start sometimes. Right when we were both new in class... feeling a bit lost maybe, trying to figure things out. I found the silliest way just to look at you.

I used to 'accidentally' drop my pen. Let it clatter and roll onto the floor. Then I'd bend down really slowly... maybe make a show of searching for it under the desk...

All just for the chance to turn my head back... just slightly... subtly... hoping to catch a glimpse of your face. Maybe hoping you were looking my way too... though I never really knew if you ever noticed my clumsy trick.

That tiny moment... the secret reason for picking up the pen... it felt like such a big deal back then. A little thrill running through me. A shy bit of hope. All just from a stolen glance across a classroom.

It feels so innocent now... remembering doing that. And so incredibly far away. Like a scene from a different life altogether. Now there's no classroom like that... no dropped pens needed as excuses... and no you sitting back there to steal a look at. Just... this quiet room. And the distant echo of that silly, hopeful feeling.

# Why You Do This To Me

It's late... my mind keeps replaying the story... maybe *our* story... like a movie reel stuck on a loop. Trying to trace the path we walked.

It started so small, Just a quiet 'maybe'. That little flicker of uncertain hope... a question mark hanging in the air between us.

Then it slowly grew into dreaming of 'some day'... imagining futures... possibilities. What could be.

And then that fragile 'something something' started happening... that connection we couldn't quite name yet, but we both felt it growing stronger between us day by day.

Until it deepened into 'something more'... becoming solid, important, undeniable. Something real.

And then... somehow... maybe quickly, maybe slowly... it felt like 'everything'. Like you were everything. Like what we had was everything that mattered. The whole world condensed into that feeling.

The whiplash came so fast after reaching that peak. Going from feeling like we finally had 'everything'... to suddenly crashing into 'not allowed'. Like a door slammed shut in our faces. Locked. Bolted. Forbidden by rules or circumstances or just... fear.

And the end result of that whole journey? From 'maybe' all the way to 'everything'? This. Just... 'nothing'. This vast, echoing quiet where 'everything' used to be just moments before.

Looking back now... the path from 'maybe' to 'nothing'... it feels dizzying. Confusing. Cruel, even. Especially that sudden, sharp fall from 'everything'. It leaves an ache that doesn't seem to fade.

# Why You Do This To Me

My own strange definition of love. It comes to mind sometimes, especially now, when it's so quiet.

It's this: Love is something that often seems like nothing much. On the surface, anyway. Quiet. Everyday. Maybe easy to overlook or take for granted sometimes. Like breathing, maybe. Seems like nothing important... just air going in and out... something you don't even notice you're doing.

But really... underneath that simple, quiet surface... it's everything. Absolutely everything. Like that air... try living without it for a minute. Suddenly that 'nothing' becomes the only thing that matters. It *is* everything. The thing you need to survive.

Was what we had like that? Did it seem like 'nothing' much sometimes... just quiet moments, comfortable silences, small shared routines? But underneath all that seeming 'nothing'... wasn't it actually holding everything together? Wasn't it... everything? To me, it felt like it was becoming that.

Now... with this emptiness... this silence... this absence... the 'nothing' it might have looked like from the outside... shows its true size. It reveals the 'everything' it really was. Just by not being here anymore. Leaving this... huge, quiet, breathless space behind where it used to be.

It's nearly 1:30 AM now... Monday morning has truly settled in. Thinking about endings... how sudden ours felt. Like a door slamming shut without any warning. No time for... proper goodbyes. And no time for one last hug.

I keep replaying our usual hugs in my mind tonight... the ones we shared almost automatically after every single meeting, right before we parted ways. That quick 3-second... maybe 5-second hold. Brief, maybe. Maybe it seemed like nothing much to an outsider. But it was *our* thing. Our little ritual of connection.

Remember how I always felt it wasn't quite long enough? Always had that little pang inside... that quiet wish for it to last just a few seconds longer as we pulled away? It always left me wanting just a little bit more of that closeness.

Funny, isn't it? Or maybe just incredibly sad. Because now, sitting here alone... I'm *still* wanting more. But what I'm so desperately wanting more of... is just *one* final chance at that moment. Just *one* more of those quick, routine, 'never quite enough' hugs. One final goodbye squeeze to hold onto.

But the end was too sudden... too sharp. It didn't allow for rituals or final moments. It just... ended. Leaving everything feeling so abrupt. So unfinished. Especially... especially that missed last hug.

# Why You Do This To Me

"I was overwhelmed," you said. "I thought some distance was better."

Distance... space... away from me. That's what you said you needed. To feel less overwhelmed, to cope.

But the confusing part... the bit that still knots up inside me whenever that memory surfaces... is that I thought I always gave you that. I thought I gave you plenty of space. Maybe even too much sometimes? I tried so hard not to crowd you. Tried to sense when you needed room to breathe and made sure to give it.

Did you not see it that way at all? Or did 'distance' mean something completely different to you? Something more... final? Something like... total separation?

Hearing you say you needed distance... when in my own head, I felt like I was already being so careful, standing respectfully back... it just didn't make sense then. And thinking about it now, here in the quiet... it still really doesn't compute. It just leaves me with this lingering, aching question... what did you really mean by 'overwhelmed'? And why wasn't the space I gave ever the right kind?

It's really late now... quiet here. Past 1:30 AM. My mind starts asking questions when it's this still. Questions I wish I could actually ask you.

Do you ever miss my touch? Just... randomly? A hand brushing yours maybe... or leaning against you? Does your skin ever remember?

Do you ever think about my eyes lingering on you? The way I sometimes couldn't help but just... watch you... taking you in?

And my voice... do you miss the sound of it? Especially when I was laughing... genuinely happy... or when you used to say you could hear the smile in my voice as we talked? That feeling you sometimes mentioned... like being wrapped up in the sound?

What about my shy 'shutup's? When I'd get embarrassed by something you said... or couldn't handle a compliment... and just mumble 'shutup' while probably blushing?

Do you miss any of those little things? Even just for a fleeting second sometimes? Or have they all just completely faded away for you now? Leaving no trace behind at all? I wonder...

# Why You Do This To Me

Thinking about that fire... that intensity we sometimes had between us. The way you used to look at me sometimes... the way you used to touch me...

It felt then like you wanted me more than anything... maybe more intensely than anyone ever had before. That raw... physical wanting. That unmistakable lust.

Does any whisper of that still exist for you? Even a tiny flicker... a hidden ember somewhere deep down? Do you ever still feel that... specific kind of desire... for me?

Or was it just... part of the story that's over now? Something that burned incredibly bright and fierce for a while... and then just... burned out completely when everything ended? Is it all just... firmly locked away in the past? Does your body even remember mine anymore in that way?

Just wondering...

"I .cherish you." And... "One thing I like about us is that I can share anything with you." Your voice saying them... I can still recall it clearly sometimes.

The sharing part... that felt so important. So real. Like a special connection we had built. No walls, no filters needed. Just open sharing.

Which makes me wonder now... Things must still be happening in your life, right? Good days, bad days, funny moments, frustrating things... the kind of stuff you would have normally told me about right away, without even thinking.

Does the urge ever hit you anymore? That old reflex... to just... share it with me? Do you ever find yourself reaching for your phone... maybe even starting to type a message... your finger hovering near where my name used to be (is it still even there?)? Thinking about telling me something... whether it's big news or just some stupid little observation?

And then... do you stop? Just... stop yourself? Delete the words? Put the phone down? Just like I find myself doing so often... that automatic reach, followed by the painful pulling back?

I wonder... is this silence just... your decision? Or are we both caught in the same sad cycle of almost reaching

# Why You Do This To Me

out and then stopping... both missing that 'share anything' connection we used to cherish? Just wondering...

Thinking about that time we talked... About the difference between being 'hot' and being 'sexy'. You asked me what I thought the difference was.

I tried to explain it... how 'sexy' felt deeper to me, more about seduction, about a feeling... like the sound of your voice, or the intensity in your eyes when you looked right at me, or the way your touch could feel. While 'hot' seemed more about just... physical appearance, something on the surface.

And then you asked me... which one I thought you were more of. Remember what I said? I said 'sexy'. Definitely more sexy than just hot. Because you had that... presence. Something really appealing and charismatic about you that went way deeper than just how you looked. You just had that certain 'something' that made your presence felt, strongly.

And sitting here now... alone in the quiet of this early morning... I realize something. That specific quality you have... the 'sexiness'... it hasn't faded in my memory, not even a little bit.

You were incredibly sexy then... when you were right here, tangible, with me. And honestly? It feels like you're still sexy now... even existing only as a memory, a feeling, a constant presence inside my head, maybe even fueled by this longing.

# Why You Do This To Me

Maybe the distance... the absence... the mystery of where you are and who you are now... maybe somehow it just amplifies that quality. Makes that charisma... that deep appeal... feel even more potent, even more magnetic from afar. More... undeniably sexy.

And maybe... that just makes you even harder to forget. Even harder to let go of.

It's late... nearly 2 AM now. Thinking about where people fit... how we mentally categorize them in our lives. Maybe like names on phone lists... friends on social media... perhaps even lists of memories tucked away.

But you... you're different. You were never just an item on a list for me. Not someone I could just... organize or file away neatly. Not someone I could delete like an old contact or check off like a finished task.

No. It's much simpler, and much more complicated than that.

You are not on my list. You are in my heart.

Lodged deep inside my chest. Like a permanent resident who doesn't need a key or permission anymore. Just... there.

And whether I want you there some days or not... that doesn't seem to change the fact. That's just where you live now. Not on paper, not on a screen that can be turned off. Right here. Always. In my heart.

# Why You Do This To Me

How... different I seem to be now. How different I feel inside, in how I face the world.

When I was with you... it felt easier, somehow. To talk honestly. To laugh freely. To show what I was really feeling deep down. You were the only one... honestly, the only one... I ever truly expressed my full self to. The good parts, the bad parts, the silly thoughts, the deep fears. It just... came out more naturally when I was with you. Like you made it safe.

Now that you're not here...? It feels like that open door inside me just slammed shut. Maybe locked itself from the inside. I feel like I'm back to being... quiet again. Guarded. That old poker face I used to wear before you... it's back firmly in place. Hard for anyone to read. Hard for anyone to get close to, probably.

It feels lonely... being this closed-off version of myself again. It makes me miss you, of course... intensely. But it also makes me miss... the 'me' that seemed to exist only when I was with you. The one who didn't always need the poker face. The one who felt safe enough to just... be.

Morning will be here in just a few hours. And like always... I know there'll be a song playing on repeat inside my head when I first wake up. Some random tune my brain decides is the soundtrack for the start of the day. It happens every single morning, like clockwork.

I don't share them anymore, though. Not with you. They're just... my private morning soundtrack now. Something I keep inside, maybe hum quietly to myself later.

But sometimes I think back... and I really miss the days when you would occasionally ask me about it. Maybe over breakfast, or in a message... "What song is stuck in your head today?" or something simple like that.

Those felt like special days when you asked. Because you asking... it wasn't just making conversation. It felt like it meant something more. It meant you were genuinely interested in that little random piece of my inner world... it meant you'd actually listen if I told you the song or played it for you. Maybe we'd even listen to it together right then, sharing that first music of the day.

Knowing you would really listen... that simple act of paying attention... it made all the difference. It made the song feel shared... connected... special. Now the songs just play on loop inside my own head... unheard by you. And every morning feels a little less special, a little more private, because of it.

# Why You Do This To Me

Remember that question you asked me once? Maybe we were talking about the future... careers, life changes, possibilities... all those hypotheticals. You asked, "By any chance in the future if we are not at the same place... you think our relationship will fade out?" We probably talked about physical distance then... how miles on a map can stretch things thin between people.

Well... look at us now. Or rather... look at where 'us' went. It did fade out, didn't it? The connection... the closeness... the easy understanding... the 'us' we were building. It's gone now. Faded completely.

But here's the ironic part... the part that twists something uncomfortable inside me when I think about it late at night like this... we are still in the same place. Still breathing the same humid air. Living in the same sprawling city, maybe just neighborhoods apart, maybe closer.

So it wasn't about the physical miles after all, was it? Your hypothetical worry... it came true. The relationship faded out. But the condition you mentioned... being in different places... it never happened.

It makes me wonder... are all relationships just destined for this? Do they all eventually fade away... whether you're near or far? Is that inevitable? Is everything just... temporary? Does closeness in miles mean nothing if the closeness in heart disappears? That thought feels incredibly heavy... and lonely... tonight.

If we ever meet again... randomly... accidentally bumping into each other somewhere in this busy city, someday down the line. How would that play out? My mind runs through the possibilities... especially when it's late and quiet like this.

Would you be the one to see me first? Would you maybe offer a small smile... say 'Hey'? Break the sudden, awkward silence that would probably hang in the air?

Or would it have to be me? Would I somehow find the nerve, the right words, to walk up to you... to initiate contact... to say something casual and normal?

Honestly... the thought of me doing that... making the first move... it feels almost impossible right now. I feel like I've forgotten how to express myself properly since we parted ways. Forgotten how to be open... how to bridge that kind of gap easily. Like that expressive part of me went dormant again, walled off.

So, I suspect what would really happen is... I'd probably just... stand there. Frozen. Rooted to the spot maybe, just watching you. Silently waiting. Hoping you'd be the one to notice me... the one to come over... the one to say the first 'Hey'.

Because what if I try, and the words come out all wrong, or worse, not at all? What if I really do have to learn all over again how to express myself... and what if someday... it just feels too difficult? Like a mountain too high to climb, just to say hello? That fear... it makes just standing there, waiting and hoping, seem like the only possible option.

I really did try to forget you. Tried quite hard for a while. I even deleted your number from my phone contacts... properly wiped it. Thought maybe if the number wasn't easily there, I wouldn't be tempted... maybe it would help create some real distance in my head too.

And the funny, almost cruel, thing is... my memory is usually terrible. Honestly, I forget important appointments, people's names minutes after hearing them, where I put my keys constantly... so many things just seem to slip right through. But your phone number? Nope. That stayed. Somehow it got burned into my brain, digit by digit. My faulty memory decided to hold onto *that*.

So, sometimes... usually when it's quiet and late like this... I find myself mentally typing the numbers out. Or maybe actually typing a text message in my notes app... words I know I'll never send. Or my thumb hovers over where the call button would be on the dial pad... just imagining pressing it... imagining hearing the ringtone... maybe hearing your voice.

But I always stop. Every single time. I pull back at the very last second. Because... I remember that I don't want to trouble you. Not anymore. You wanted space, or things ended for a reason, and I need to respect that boundary. Troubling your peace feels wrong.

So I just... put the phone down. Let the impulse pass. And sit with the feeling that remains instead. This quiet, persistent ache. This specific kind of melancholy that wraps around me in these moments.

And sometimes... maybe it sounds strange to admit, even just to myself... but sometimes this melancholic feeling itself... it feels almost... familiar. Even comfortable, in a weird way? Like putting on an old, worn-out sweater that's full of sad memories but still feels known. Like a sad song I know all the words to by heart. Maybe... maybe I just love the feeling because it's still *a* feeling connected to you.

It's quiet now... really quiet. Past 2:15 AM. The kind of deep quiet that sometimes makes you remember sounds... good sounds from the past. Like music playing in the car during those long drives we used to take together.

Maybe heading out of the city late at night... windows down sometimes... the breeze rushing in, carrying the faint sounds of the road. And the songs... our little ritual we had. It was always your turn first... you'd pick one of your absolute favorite tracks. Then it would be my turn... and I'd play one of mine. Back and forth like that, for miles. Sharing the music that shaped us... the songs we loved for different reasons.

It felt like more than just listening to music together. It felt like a conversation... happening without needing words. Just sharing pieces of ourselves... our feelings... our histories... through the melodies and lyrics we chose. Like we were understanding each other a little bit more with each track played.

That feeling... that easy connection built on shared sound, shared journeys... it feels so incredibly far away right now. Compared to this deep silence. And just now... this sudden, strong wave of nostalgia washed over me... for those drives, for that ritual, for the simple back-and-forth of sharing our favorite songs with you. Just... missing it.

# Why You Do This To Me

Sometimes, when I'm walking through the rush, I find myself looking at the faces passing by. My eyes might glance at the girls walking past... not in a weird way, definitely not checking them out... it's more like... just observing humanity, I guess. Seeing all these different lives crossing mine for a split second.

And a question always seems to pop into my head in those moments: Could I ever connect with someone new like *that* again? Could I ever find that same feeling... that same deep understanding... that instant 'click' I felt when I first really connected with you? Is that specific kind of connection even possible twice in a lifetime?

But my heart... or maybe just my cynical brain these days... it always answers immediately, before I can even really start to hope. The answer feels like it's always 'No'.

What we had... what I felt with you... it just feels different in my memory. Unique. Unrepeatable. Maybe it *was* truly a once-in-a-lifetime kind of connection. And accepting that possibility... accepting that the answer inside me is always 'no'... it feels heavy. It makes the crowded world feel a little lonelier, and a little less bright.

Remember that first day we really talked? Properly talked? In the canteen... supposed to be about some project, wasn't it? Seems like a whole different lifetime ago now.

I remember seeing you clearly... noticing a tiny ant exploring the collar of your slightly crumpled shirt. I remember you trying to look confident and composed, but maybe feeling a bit new or nervous underneath too.

We were only supposed to talk for a few minutes... finish the project discussion quickly. But somehow... it stretched into two whole hours. Just like that. Time completely dissolved around us. I remember actively not wanting it to end... not wanting you to leave.

When I finally had to pull myself away to go finish my work, I remember rushing back to the canteen afterwards... heart pounding a little, foolishly maybe... hoping against hope you might still be there, maybe lingering or waiting. But you were gone.

Did you feel it too, that day? That sudden spark? That unexpected connection forming so fast between two people who barely knew each other? It felt like something *significant* was happening... something I hadn't felt in such a long, long time. What did you do to my heart right from that very first proper meeting? What *is* this connection that still echoes so strongly now, even after all this time and distance? I still don't really know.

# Why You Do This To Me

This silly thought comes back to me sometimes... usually when **I**'m feeling the weight of all the unanswered questions from that time. My mind goes straight back to that first day in the canteen... and to that tiny ant making its journey across **your** shirt collar.

And **I** think... what if **I** could have been that small? That insignificant to the world, but close enough to know everything? **I** wish, with a strange kind of ache, that **I** could have been that little ant.

**I** would have just clung on... stayed with **you** silently, unseen, when **you** stood up and walked away from the table, away from me. **I** would have gone wherever **you** went next, a secret passenger. And **I** would have tried to listen... not to the sounds of the city outside... but to the quiet, hidden sounds of **your** thoughts. To what **you** were *really* thinking right after **we** parted.

Then **I** would have known, wouldn't **I**? Known for sure if **you** were thinking about me too... if **your** heart was also buzzing with that same surprising, unexpected connection that mine was. **I** would have known, right from that very first moment, if the magic was real for **you** too.

It's such a strange, childish wish... to want to be an ant. But sometimes, it feels like that's the only way **I** could ever get the one thing **I** still crave from that very first day: the simple, beautiful certainty of knowing.

The time I walked into that cafe... the one we sometimes went to? My eyes were scanning all the tables... looking only for you.

And then I saw you. Sitting by the window maybe... or tucked into a corner booth... before you even noticed I'd arrived.

You were wearing that white oversized shirt you liked... those comfy, soft baggy jeans. Your head was bent over a book... completely absorbed in whatever world was on the pages. And your long hair was untied... falling down like a dark curtain, partly hiding your face as you read, catching the light.

Just seeing you like that... in that simple, unguarded moment... completely lost in your own world... unaware I was watching... you looked so incredibly beautiful. Stunning, actually. In a quiet, effortless way that words felt completely inadequate for... both then and now. Just... perfectly, breathtakingly beautiful.

That specific picture of you... it's still so clear in my memory. Sharp and vivid. Like a photograph saved permanently inside my head. A sight I wish desperately I could just stumble upon and see for real again.

# Why You Do This To Me

Here I am again. Sitting in a coffee shop... not our old one, just some random place I ducked into this evening. The light is fading outside, the place is busy, people are talking, the machine is grinding beans... but all that noise just seems to make the quietness inside my own head feel louder. It's just... not the same.

My mind drifts back, easily, to that little place near the college, remember? How we'd manage to find a corner table. The world outside, even the rest of the cafe around us, could be buzzing with chaos... but we always managed to create this invisible bubble just around our table. A little sanctuary for the two of us.

Inside that bubble, the conversation was so easy. It would wander anywhere it wanted to go... from deep thoughts about life and the future to the silliest, most pointless jokes that only we found funny. We talked about everything and we talked about nothing, all at once. There was never any pressure. Just an easy, comfortable flow between us, like we were speaking our own private language.

I miss that. Terribly. I miss looking up from my cup and just... seeing you there. Right across the table... listening... maybe smiling a little.

I just took a sip of my coffee... and it tastes exactly how I feel. Lonely. It's strange how a simple cup of coffee can taste so much like a memory... and even more, so much like an absence.

Our unspoken rule, right from the beginning, was always no holding hands in public. We both seemed to agree without ever saying it... that it was all a bit much, too much for show. A 'public display of affection', when what we felt seemed so perfectly private, so uniquely ours.

But we had our own way of being close. Walking down the promenade by the sea at night... with the sound of the waves crashing softly nearby... we'd walk so near to each other. Just close enough that a misstep or a change in pace would make our shoulders brush together. A tiny, fleeting point of contact that honestly felt more intimate, more real, than holding hands ever could.

Our connection lived in the air between us... filled with the constant flow of conversation... easy laughter that mixed with the salty sea breeze... pointing out silly things in the dark, or just being quiet together, knowing the other person was right there.

That was our brand of closeness. Strong. Confident. It didn't need to be declared to the world with intertwined fingers. It was real, and it was just for us.

I walk those same routes alone sometimes, like this evening. The sea sounds the same, the breeze feels the same. But the space beside me is just... empty air now. And I find myself missing that specific feeling with an intensity that surprises me. I miss the kind of closeness

that was so strong, so certain, it didn't need to be held to
be felt.

*A silent, knowing touch*

Driving alone late sometimes... maybe stuck in traffic, maybe on an empty road... an old Hindi song comes on the radio. Kishore Kumar... Lata... maybe an old RD Burman tune. Instantly... I'm back in the car with you. Windows down perhaps... the city lights a warm blur outside. You humming along... maybe singing the wrong lyrics and laughing. Those songs felt different then... shared. Nostalgic, yes, but a happy, shared nostalgia. Now when they play... they just sound purely nostalgic... and bring this wave of sadness. Miss those drives. Miss our specific old-song soundtrack.

# Why You Do This To Me

That college canteen... it was always so bright and loud and chaotic. Amidst all that noise... I remember sometimes just looking across the crowded table... and catching you smiling. Maybe at something funny someone said... maybe just a quiet smile at your own thoughts... maybe even at me. Just that quick, genuine curve of your lips. It always lit up your whole face. And usually, it lit up my entire day too. Catching that unexpected smile... it felt like finding something precious in the middle of chaos. Haven't seen a smile quite like it since then.

Our coffee shop conversations... they could roam anywhere. Deep philosophical debates one minute... planning impossible futures... dissecting movie plots... then descending into absolute nonsense and laughter the next. No topic felt off-limits. No judgment in your eyes. Just... talking. Listening. Exploring ideas together. Hearing your unique way of seeing things. Sharing mine. Feels like I haven't had a real conversation like that... that free, that open, that stimulating... in such a long time. The silence now feels... heavy. Stifling, almost.

# Why You Do This To Me

For years... maybe my whole life before you... I was almost proud of it, in a strange way. My skill. The ability to just... switch off emotionally. If any feeling started to get too warm... too close to what I thought love might be... nope. Shut it down immediately. Change the channel in my head. Focus hard on work, on distractions... anything else. Avoid it. Suppress it. And honestly... after years of practice... it became easy. Almost automatic. Love wasn't for me, I'd tell myself. Didn't understand it, probably wasn't capable of it, didn't really want it anyway.

But you... somehow you changed the frequency. The feeling I had when I was with you... that connection, that warmth, that ease... whatever label it deserved... it felt... different. Good. Real. Like something I didn't want to switch off, for the very first time ever. I actually wanted to lean into it, explore it, let it be.

And now... this feeling. This deep, quiet melancholy of missing you. It's heavy, yes. It definitely aches, especially right now, in these still hours just before dawn breaks over Mumbai. But the strangest thing is happening. I find I don't want to run from this feeling either. The old instinct to switch off, to numb it out... it's there, faintly... but I don't want to follow it.

It feels like... proof, maybe. Proof that what I felt with you was real... that I am capable of feeling deeply after all. And maybe... maybe I'd rather sit here with this specific sadness... this melancholy that's so clearly tied to you and the love I felt... than go back to that old, easy numbness, that state of feeling nothing much at all.

So I'll just... stay with it for now. Let this melancholy keep me company in the quiet. It feels more honest, somehow. More real.

# Why You Do This To Me

It's so quiet now... 4:19 AM. Still dark outside before the dawn even thinks about breaking. Thinking about... 'bonus days'. Remember that silly name we might have had for them? Or maybe it was just a name I gave them in my own head. Those specific, wonderful days...

They were the ones when you'd just... surprise me. Completely out of the blue... maybe a soft 'I love you' whispered for no particular reason at all, just because you felt it. Or a quick, unexpected kiss stolen while we were busy doing something else entirely, like cooking or just passing each other in the hallway. Or sometimes you'd say something simple... something completely insightful or sweet that I never saw coming... maybe something you noticed about me... and it would just perfectly melt my heart right there in that moment.

Those days felt like... finding hidden treasure when you weren't even looking. Like getting a wonderful, unexpected gift that made everything around seem brighter, warmer. They weren't every single day... maybe that's precisely why they felt like such special bonuses when they did happen.

God, I miss those bonus days. Terribly. I miss the element of sweet surprise... the spontaneous warmth... the feeling of being so seen and cherished that came wrapped up inside those little, unexpected moments. It feels like it's been such a long, long time without a bonus day now. Just... ordinary days stretching on.

Sometimes, even now... when I'm walking down a busy street... I'll suddenly remember something funny you said or did way back when. And a smile will almost... almost... start to form on my face. Reflex. But then the awareness hits... I'm alone. And you're not there to share the memory with... not there to smile back. The impulse fades before it even truly begins. It makes me think... like your smile I miss seeing... maybe my own smiles need you nearby to fully come alive too.

# Why You Do This To Me

Driving alone at night now feels... hollow. The silence inside the car is a heavy thing. It always reminds me of how it used to be... how it felt when you were here beside me.

Some of our most honest, most real conversations unfolded in that small space, didn't they? Maybe it was the magic of being 'trapped' together, moving as one through the dark city. The world outside was just a passing blur of lights and shadows... and inside, it felt like it was only us. Maybe it was the lack of pressure... not having to look directly at each other... that allowed the truth to finally come out more easily.

That car became a confessional. A sanctuary on wheels. Quiet confessions were whispered into the space between us, secrets that I doubt had ever been spoken out loud before. Big, impossible dreams were built, seeming almost real and achievable in that bubble. We'd share silly observations about passing billboards, things only funny to us. It was in those moments, in that little moving room, that all the walls seemed to just... dissolve.

It wasn't just a car then. It was our little mobile world... a safe space where we could be completely, vulnerably honest with each other without fear.

I miss that bubble with an ache so deep it surprises me sometimes. It's not just the drives I miss... or even just the talks themselves. I miss the profound *safety* of that space with you. The rare feeling of being able to say anything...

and knowing, truly knowing, that I was being heard and understood.

That feeling... it's gone. And now the car is just a car again. The silence is just silence. And the loneliness on these drives feels... vast.

# Why You Do This To Me

Your question just echoed in my head... popping up out of nowhere this afternoon, right in the middle of a normal Tuesday. *"Is this relationship getting shallow?"* Remember asking me that? The words hung heavy in the air then... confusing me, maybe hurting a little more than I let on.

It made me think, both then and now... what *is* a shallow relationship, really? What does that feeling actually mean? Does it feel... like this? This hollow ache I carry around constantly now... this profound emptiness where you and *us* used to be? Is *this* feeling I have now... this void... is *this* the shallowness you were talking about back then? Is it possible you felt this kind of emptiness... even when I was right there with you?

If you did feel that way... why? I remember asking you why you felt it was getting shallow... I asked you several times, really trying to understand what was missing for you. But you never really answered me. Never gave me a clear reason I could hold onto or try to fix.

Were you maybe looking for something more concrete from me? A logical list of reasons *why* I was with you, why I liked you, why I loved you? Trying perhaps to find a logic that, for me at least, simply wasn't there? Because I think I told you then, and it's still true now... I never had a neat list of reasons for loving you. It wasn't built on logic. It was just... a feeling. A deep, undeniable connection. Reasonless. Constant.

Now... all I have left is the lingering memory of your unanswered question... and this vast, undeniable shallowness where our deep connection used to be. *This* emptiness I feel now... *this* feels shallow. What we had didn't. Not to me. Never to me.

# Why You Do This To Me

Whenever I hear one of those truly classic romantic Hindi songs now... the kind we both loved and used to play on those drives... the first image that comes to mind is your smile. Can't help it. I feel like you had a specific smile reserved for those melodies sometimes... maybe softer? More thoughtful? A little nostalgic itself? Or maybe I'm just layering my own feelings onto the memory now. But the songs and your smile... they're completely tangled together in my head. Makes listening very bittersweet. Beautiful music... painful reminder.

It's late now... nearly 2:40 AM. Thinking about simple things... like the feeling of a warm mug in your hands on a cooler night. Thinking about you... and the way you used to drink hot chocolate.

Specifically... I keep picturing the expression on your face. Right after you took the first proper sip from the mug. That little look that would just flicker across your features for a moment...

Was it pure contentment settling in? A little surprise maybe, at the sweetness or the comforting heat? Maybe a mix of both? It's actually hard to put exact words to it, looking back. But I remember it so clearly in my mind's eye. How your eyes might have closed just for a fraction of a second... maybe a tiny, almost silent, satisfied sigh escaped your lips.

It feels like it's been such a long, long time since I saw that look for real. Ages.

I used to love watching for it. Seeing that simple, unguarded moment of pleasure or comfort wash over you. I honestly felt, in those moments, like I could just sit there quietly and look at you with that specific expression forever... and never, ever get bored or look away. Just... watch you be content, forever.

I miss that simple moment. I miss seeing that particular look on your face more than I can say.

# Why You Do This To Me

A new kind of worry hit me tonight... the fear that the specific details are starting to fade. The exact shade of your eyes in the sunlight... the specific musical sound of your laugh... the precise feeling of your hand brushing mine. I try to hold onto them tightly in my mind... picture them clearly... but they feel like watercolor paintings left out in the rain. Blurring at the edges. Forgetting those details feels like losing you all over again... a slower, quieter kind of loss.

Woke up this morning... there was the usual random song playing in my head. Made coffee the same way I always do. Went through the motions. The routine feels... safe. Grounding. But it also feels hollow now. Because the routine used to include... the possibility of a message from you... or the thought of telling you about the funny song in my head later. Now it's just... actions. Motions. Without the shared meaning that gave them warmth.

# Why You Do This To Me

Seeing couples out and about... maybe laughing together over coffee... or just walking quietly side-by-side down the street (sometimes not even holding hands, just comfortable in each other's presence, like we used to be)... it brings this sudden, sharp pang. A visceral reminder of that easy companionship. That feeling of having your person moving through the world beside you. I find myself looking away quickly now. It just highlights what's missing.

All these thoughts... these reflections... these questions... these unsent messages piling up inside my head and my heart... they feel physically heavy sometimes. Like carrying around a backpack full of stones. Words I maybe should have said back then? Words I desperately want to say now but can't? Words that simply have nowhere to go. Just weighing me down in the ongoing silence.

# Why You Do This To Me

Took a drive earlier tonight... couldn't sleep. Just circled the quieter Mumbai streets after midnight. Put on some of those old Hindi songs we loved. But it wasn't the same at all. The passenger seat felt enormous... achingly empty. The music sounded hollow, somehow. The magic wasn't just in the drive or the songs... it was always in having you there beside me, sharing it.

*The empty seat*

Sometimes, my mind becomes a small, dark movie theater... and there's only one film it ever wants to play. The last scene. The final one with you.

I play it over and over again, especially in quiet moments like this evening. Our last real conversation... or maybe that final time I saw you properly, before everything changed. I rewind it. I watch it in slow motion. I try to zoom in on your face in my memory, desperately trying to see something new this time around. Was there a flicker in your eyes? A tightness around your mouth? A slight hesitation in your words that I was just too blind or too hopeful to notice back then? Was there some tiny sign of what was coming that I completely missed?

Then I turn the lens on myself. I analyze my own lines, my own actions in the scene. Did I say the wrong thing right at that crucial moment? Was my timing off? Did I miss my cue to say something important... something that might have changed the entire ending of the film? Or did I simply not say enough when I had the chance?

But no matter how many times I rewatch it, the ending is always the same. It just... ends. Abruptly. And I'm left sitting alone in the dark of my own mind, searching for answers, for clues, for deleted scenes that probably don't even exist. Just an endless, looping film of questions with no director's cut to explain it all.

# Why You Do This To Me

Traffic... Everyone hates it, right? It's practically a city-wide pastime to complain about the endless waiting... the noise... the sheer frustration of being stuck.

But I remember... back then... when I was with you... maybe stuck in the car together, or inching along painfully slow on a bike amidst that sea of vehicles... I didn't mind it at all. Honestly? I think I secretly loved it sometimes.

Because every red light that seemed to last forever... every slow, frustrating crawl down the flyover or through a choked lane... it just meant... more time. Unexpected bonus minutes gifted to us.

More time to simply sit beside you. More time to talk... or listen to music... or just be quiet together comfortably, watching the city move slowly around us. More time where maybe I could reach over and take your hand. More time, crucially, before we reached wherever we were going... before we had to part ways.

Now? When I get stuck in traffic alone... it's just traffic again. Exactly what everyone complains about. Annoying. Stressful. A waste of precious time. The magic ingredient that transformed the experience – you – is missing from the seat beside me.

And I really, deeply miss the days when just your presence could make even a terrible Mumbai traffic jam feel... like a small, secret, welcome gift of a few more moments together.

Remember those late-night phone calls? When the whole city was finally asleep... just our voices whispering back and forth across the line. Sometimes talking about deep, important things... sometimes just sitting in comfortable silence together, hearing each other breathe. My phone feels so cold and silent at this hour now. Miss the warmth of your voice filling the late-night quiet.

# Why You Do This To Me

The glow of the phone screen is the only light in the room this evening. My thumbs moved on their own, almost from muscle memory... tapping out a whole message to **you**. A long one... sentence by careful sentence. I watched the words appear on the screen, a little island of things I wish I could say.

Then, just as methodically, I erased them. The backspace button became a tiny digital executioner... deleting it all, letter by letter, until the screen was blank and quiet again. The urge returned almost immediately... maybe just a simple, harmless 'Hey'? But my thumb froze over the keypad. I just couldn't press send.

It truly feels like there's an invisible wall between us now. A high, thick wall built out of unspoken words, maybe of hurt feelings, maybe just of time and distance. And each letter I type feels like trying to throw a tiny pebble over that massive wall... knowing it will probably just fall short, unheard. It feels pointless.

I miss the days when there were no walls. When the path between us was clear and open. When messages just... flowed. An easy, thoughtless back-and-forth without this heavy weight, without this deep hesitation. That easy path... it's gone now. Replaced by this wall. And a blank, silent screen.

The silence in this room feels enormous tonight. Crushing, almost. It used to be filled... with our conversations... your unique laugh... the background music we'd play... even just the quiet sound of you being nearby, reading or working. Now... it's just pure silence. And the loud echo of everything that's missing.

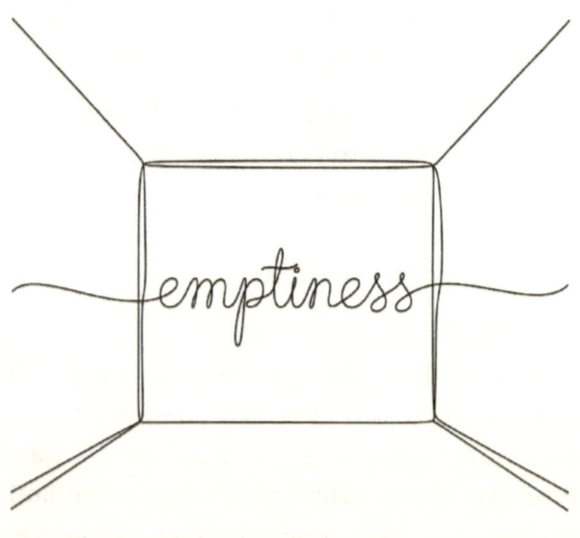

# Why You Do This To Me

Saw your profile picture somewhere online earlier... just popped up unexpectedly on a mutual friend's feed or something. Just that tiny little thumbnail image. My heart did that stupid, painful lurch it does. Just seeing your face... even a tiny, static, smiling version... brought everything rushing back in a wave. I scrolled past as fast as I could. Some sights are just too painful right now.

Found myself playing that one specific old Hindi song on repeat for an hour tonight. The one you first made me listen to on one of those long drives. Each time the melody restarts, it feels like I'm trying to recapture something... a feeling... that specific moment in time. But it doesn't work. It just makes the present emptiness feel stronger in contrast.

# Why You Do This To Me

Something happened today... a small, silly thing... that instantly reminded me of one of our ridiculous inside jokes. I almost laughed out loud on the street... then caught myself. Looked around. Realized there was nobody with me who would understand the reference. It felt surprisingly lonely... having a whole secret language of jokes that only one other person understands... and that person isn't here to share the laugh with.

My mind has this habit... especially in quiet moments like this evening... of replaying old, fleeting scenes. And one of the clips it plays most often is the memory of **your** face in a quiet moment. Specifically... the exact way **you** used to look at me sometimes when **you** thought **I** wasn't paying attention.

**Your** usual guard would drop for just a second, and this softer, completely unguarded expression would just... appear. Looking back, that specific look now feels like a beautiful, intricate puzzle **I** was handed... one that came with no solution, and one **I'm** still trying to solve now. It feels like trying to read a sentence written in a language **I** almost knew, but never fully learned.

What was it saying? Was the language one of quiet, deep affection? Was it gentle curiosity? Or just simple, fond amusement at something **I'd** done or said? Each time **I** replay the memory, **I** try a different translation. **I** examine every detail **I** can recall... the slight curve of **your** lips, the specific light in **your** eyes... searching desperately for a clue, for a key to finally decipher its meaning.

But it's a useless exercise, isn't it? Trying to translate a feeling from the past without the person who felt it. **I'm** left here, years later maybe, still trying to solve the beautiful, fleeting puzzle of **your** expression... knowing with a quiet ache that it's far, far too late to just look at **you**, smile, and ask the simplest question of all: "What are **you** thinking?"

# Why You Do This To Me

"The Silent Patient"... that was the book you were reading. The very first time we met properly, sitting across from each other in that cafe. I remember seeing the cover clearly. It feels deeply ironic now, doesn't it? Thinking about that title... and then thinking about the profound silence that stretches between us now.

Sometimes, especially late at night like this... when my mind won't quiet down... I wish I could be like a detective in a book. Investigate the whole situation... find the real, concrete reason for *this* silence... for why you disappeared from my life so completely. Put all the clues and memories together and finally, finally understand the 'why'.

But then I hesitate. A part of me pulls back. Because... what if the real reason isn't some big, dramatic mystery? What if it's... small? Or petty? Or just... crushingly ordinary and disappointing? Maybe even hurtful in a way I haven't even considered yet?

I've spun so many different stories in my own head over time, trying to make sense of it all. Different scenarios, different reasons for why you left, why things ended. And I can't help but wonder... maybe some of those made-up reasons actually feel... *better*? Kinder, somehow? More bearable to live with than whatever the actual, unvarnished truth might really be?

Perhaps keeping the mystery... letting the central 'why' remain unanswered... is a strange kind of self-protection.

Maybe, deep down, I prefer my own fiction to a potentially harsh reality. Maybe sometimes... it really is better to be the silent patient myself. Just holding onto stories and interpretations... instead of digging for cold, hard facts that might break things inside me even more.

# Why You Do This To Me

Remember all those 'some day' plans we used to talk about? Trips we'd take... things we wanted to try together... future dreams, big and small? They float around in my head like little ghosts sometimes... painful reminders of a shared future that isn't going to happen now. Each remembered plan feels like a tiny, unexpected stab.

Thinking today... about words left unsaid. Why didn't I just say it more often when I had the chance? Those simple, huge words... 'I love you.' Or even just, 'I need you.' Or, 'I really want you here with me.' Seems so straightforward when you write it down like this.

But my logic back then, my firmly held belief, was always... if the feeling between two people is real, truly real and deep, then it should just be *understood*. It should be felt, like an energy, a current running between them. I thought it shouldn't need constant verbal confirmation. Saying the words felt... almost less important than the undeniable feeling itself. I thought the connection we had spoke much louder and more clearly than any simple phrase could.

But now... looking back on everything with these eyes, from this quiet distance... I see it differently. I realize that maybe *you* needed to hear the words sometimes. Maybe words aren't just words after all. Maybe for the person hearing them, they act like anchors... like reassurance... like tangible proof of the feeling. Something they can hold onto, especially when things feel uncertain. Maybe saying it wasn't important for *me*... but maybe it was crucial for *you* to hear.

And maybe... if I'm being completely honest with myself right now... maybe I was also just scared. Scared that saying something so big, so vulnerable – words I used so rarely, words that meant so much *because* I used them so rarely – what if I finally said them, finally poured my heart out... and then you left anyway? Wouldn't that break the power, the meaning of those precious words? Wouldn't it make the feeling itself feel... devalued? Exposed and rejected?

So I often kept quiet. Held back the explicit words, even when the feeling was practically shouting inside my chest. Until perhaps... the silence stretched on too long... became too comfortable for me, maybe, and too empty for you.

And when I finally *did* say it... finally found the courage, or perhaps the desperation pushed me... maybe the moment had already passed between us. Maybe the echo just came... too late. That possibility... that my fear and my silence cost us everything... it's a heavy one to carry around.

Which is why, I suppose, I'm writing it all down now... in this book. Pouring out all the things I couldn't say then. It's where the words can finally exist, finally take shape... even if they still don't ever reach you.

Found an old scarf tucked away in the back of the cupboard... I think it still faintly smells like you... or maybe it's just the memory of your scent clinging to it, mixing with the dust. I held it for just a moment. Like trying to hold onto smoke. Quickly put it back. Some memories feel too sharp, too real to touch for long.

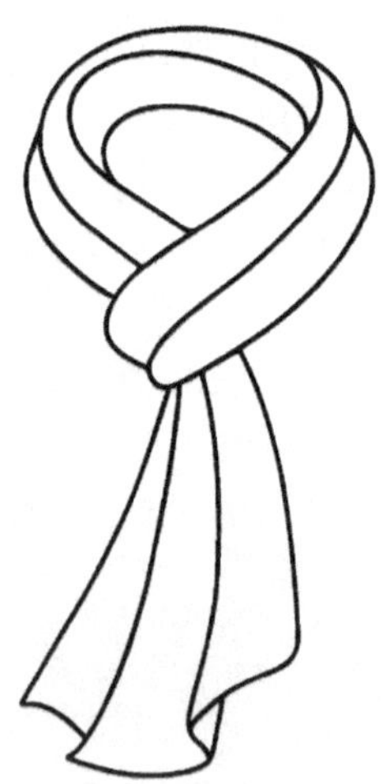

# Why You Do This To Me

Sometimes... when it's really late and quiet like this... I find myself foolishly, desperately wishing for some kind of sign. Any sign at all. That you think of me too, even occasionally. That you miss this connection too. A random message that makes no sense... seeing your name unexpectedly... a song lyric that seems pointedly meant for me... anything. But the silence just stretches on. Unbroken.

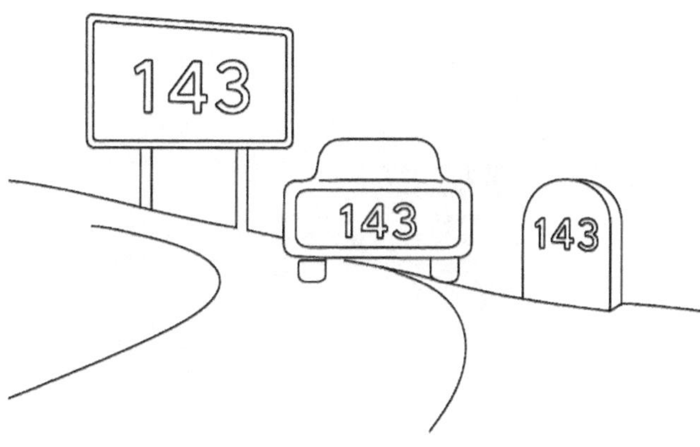

Found myself scrolling way back... through old chat logs tonight (the ones I couldn't bring myself to delete). Reading your words... reading my own words back to you. Searching for clues... hidden meanings... warnings I completely missed at the time. Were the answers to why it ended hiding there in plain sight all along? Or am I just torturing myself by digging through digital ruins? Probably the latter.

# Why You Do This To Me

It's strange... how feelings work sometimes. How they show up on your face... or maybe now... how they don't. It's past 1 AM now... the quietest time, good for these strange thoughts.

I was just remembering that day in class... when we ended up sitting next to each other. That silly, uncontrollable smile I had on my face just because you were right there, breathing the same air. Remember the teacher asking me why I was smiling? I think I lied... mumbled something like 'Oh, I just have a smiling face'. Which wasn't true... the smile was all because you were next to me.

Just now... thinking about you, about that memory... I felt that same lightness bubble up inside again. A definite smile blooming somewhere in my mind, in my feelings. But I happened to glance in the mirror a moment ago... and saw nothing. No smile on my actual face. Just... me. Looking tired, maybe.

Why is that? Why does the thought of you still create the feeling deep inside... that warmth, that urge to smile... but it doesn't travel to my face anymore? Is it because the source... the reason for the smile... isn't physically here? Because you're a memory now... a thought living in my head... not a real presence sitting right here beside me?

It makes the missing feel... different somehow. Sharper, maybe. Knowing that even my own face refuses to pretend you're still here... making me smile without me even knowing it.

My brain is doing loops again... thinking about expressing feelings... how hard it can be sometimes. How hard it often felt for me... especially with you.

I always seemed to get it wrong, didn't I? Either I'd say almost nothing... keeping all the important feelings locked up tight inside. Or, the opposite – the feelings would burst out suddenly... and I'd say way too much, probably sounding over-the-top... maybe even like some 'filmy flirt', like you couldn't take it seriously. Not like the real, simple feeling inside. Not like me.

I think... back then... I just hoped you would somehow know. Understand the things I couldn't quite put into simple words. I hoped you could read the real feeling behind my awkward silences... or maybe see through the flood of clumsy words if I accidentally said too much. Just... understand me.

But what if you didn't? What if you couldn't read my mind... or my heart? What if you actually needed to hear the words? Said clearly? Simply? Directly?

What if you were waiting for plain, honest words that I never managed to find or speak out loud? Could that be it? Could that be the simple, stupid reason why everything eventually fell apart between us? Because I couldn't bridge that gap... between what I felt so strongly inside... and the right words I failed to give you?

That thought... wondering if it was my failure with words... it keeps me awake sometimes. Like tonight.

# Why You Do This To Me

It's late... quiet balcony weather tonight. The kind of night that pulls old memories to the surface. It makes me remember that night... on a balcony... maybe one just like this one, overlooking the sleeping city.

Remember? You were sitting right on my lap... leaning close against me. Heavy and warm. How there was absolutely no space left between us in that moment. Skin touching... breathing the same rhythm of the night air. Just... complete closeness.

I remember looking up at your face... seeing the curve of your smile there in the dim light... I remember my hand holding yours... tracing patterns on your skin... playing with your long fingers.

What were we talking about? I try so hard sometimes to remember the words... the actual conversation... but they're gone. Completely vanished into the past.

But I remember that feeling. Perfectly. The total absence of distance between us. Physical... emotional... it felt like all the usual walls and defenses just dissolved for a little while. It was just us. Existing together in that tiny bubble of shared time and space... safe... connected... away from the whole noisy world.

It felt... infinite then. Like that closeness could last forever. Now... there feels like nothing but space between us. An ocean of quiet distance stretching out. Remembering that specific moment when there was absolutely no space... it's such a beautiful, vivid memory. But tonight... thinking about it... it just hurts. A deep, quiet hurt.

# Why You Do This To Me

You're always on my mind... my thoughts just circle back to you, again and again. That's easy to notice.

And you're always in my heart... that familiar mix of ache and warmth is right there, a constant pulse. I feel that clearly too.

But it feels like there's more than that... like you're somewhere else inside me too. Somewhere deeper down. A place I can't quite name or understand properly. Like you're just woven into the very fabric of who I am now, beyond just thoughts and feelings.

Mind, heart... and this quiet, constant presence somewhere deeper still. It feels like you're just... part of me. Everywhere.

I have full conversations with you in my head sometimes. Ridiculous, isn't it? Telling you all about my day... asking your opinion on something... arguing with you about a movie... reacting to the replies I imagine you giving. It feels strangely comforting for a fleeting moment... like you're still here to talk to. And then the silence crashes back in, and it feels deeply, profoundly lonely. Like I'm just talking to a ghost that only I can see.

# Why You Do This To Me

This city... it still looks the same, mostly. Still sounds the same... the traffic, the vendors, the sea. But it feels completely different without you being an active part of my life in it (even though you're physically still here somewhere). The places we used to go... that specific cafe, that stretch of beach, that bookstore... they feel haunted now. Filled with ghosts of memories that make them hard to revisit without feeling this ache.

Even after everything... after the sudden ending, after the 'not allowed', after settling into this 'nothing'... sometimes that tiny, initial flicker of 'maybe' still returns. A foolish, completely illogical spark of hope ignites in the dark. What if someday... somehow... things could be different...? It's usually extinguished by cold reality within seconds. But the fact that the 'maybe' can still spark at all, even for a moment... it just shows how deep this connection went. Or perhaps... how stubborn my heart refuses to be.

# Why You Do This To Me

Maybe it's true, what I was thinking before... sometimes the stories we tell ourselves *are* better, or at least easier to live with, than the actual story, the hard reality. Like maybe my guesses about why you left are kinder than the real reason might be.

But the *other* kind of stories... the ones we used to build *together*... just by talking... they were definitely, absolutely better than this silence is now. God, I loved those conversations we used to have. Especially the really deep ones... the intellectual ones, where we weren't afraid to really dive in.

Remember how we'd take an idea... or something that happened... or something about people... and just dissect it for hours? Turn it over and over... looking at it from your perspective... then exploring it from mine... really trying to understand things more deeply, more fully, together? I felt like I learned so much just from seeing the world through your eyes in those talks.

I still think like that... those kinds of analyses, those mental 'stories' about how things work or why people are the way they are... they still form constantly in my head. It's how my brain works. But the person I want to discuss them with... the person I want to debate with... the person I want to explore them with... you... you're not here to do that with anymore.

And what good is developing these thoughts, these perspectives, these stories, if there's no one to share them with in that specific, challenging, yet understanding way we had? They just end up bouncing around uselessly inside my own skull, with no echo, no response.

So... the only thing to do, it seems most days... is to try and forget them. To stop the thoughts as soon as they start getting interesting. To push the stories away before they fully form. To try and move on from needing that kind of shared intellectual spark, that back-and-forth. But it's hard work. And I really, truly miss thinking things through *with you*. That specific connection... it's irreplaceable.

# Why You Do This To Me

The sky outside will start changing color soon, shifting from black to grey. And I'm lying here awake, wondering... sometimes worrying a little... how do you sleep now?

I remember our nightly ritual so clearly. We'd talk... maybe on the phone, maybe just texting back and forth... until your replies started getting slower... sleepier. Then, just before signing off, I'd always say it... 'Good night... I've hugged you tight'. And even though we weren't physically together then, I always felt a real connection in that moment, like I really *was* sending that comfort across the distance. I used to picture you drifting off to sleep peacefully after that... feeling safe... carefree.

Was that feeling real? Did I actually help you sleep better? Or is *this* the actual reality – you, sleeping perfectly fine every night without my good nights, without that imagined hug? Maybe it made no difference at all?

Or... has someone else taken my place in that ritual? Does someone else whisper goodnight to you now, offer you comfort as you fall asleep? Is it even *possible* for someone else to slip into that specific, quiet, end-of-day space I thought was uniquely ours? Was I... was what I offered... that easily replaceable? Like swapping out one worn part for a new one?

Or maybe... maybe the story I try to tell myself sometimes, the kinder story, is the truth? Maybe you're just strong enough now. Sleeping peacefully and soundly all on your own... not needing anyone's words or imagined hugs to feel safe as you drift off.

I go back and forth between hoping you're okay alone... and the sharp sting of fearing I was replaced, or maybe never really mattered that much in the first place. It's confusing... lying here wondering about your sleep, when I often can't find my own.

# Why You Do This To Me

It's difficult tonight. So incredibly difficult. And it hurts... a deep, relentless kind of ache that settles in the chest and makes it hard to breathe.

My mind is so loud in the quiet of this early morning. A million thoughts just circling... the same questions replaying over and over, finding no new answers. It feels like this pain will just... stretch on forever. Like when I try to look ahead, into the future, there's nothing to see but darkness. A thick, heavy curtain.

There's a quiet voice inside that whispers it might not make it through this time. A part of me that questions if it's even worth the fight to try.

I know tonight is hard. Tomorrow will probably be hard too. And the night after that... maybe it will be just the same.

But then... another thought surfaces, faintly. A distant memory. I've been here before. Not in this exact way, maybe, but in this same place of hurting. And somehow... somehow, I survived it then.

There must be some strength left inside me from those other times. There must be. I have to believe that. I have to believe that just like all the times before... I can get through this. That someday, eventually, I will get over this.

Maybe... just maybe... I will be fine again.

Maybe... I will be okay.

# Until Maybe...

So, we've reached the last page. But the thoughts... the feelings... they don't always end so neatly, do they? The memories still surface unexpectedly, the questions still echo in the quiet hours, and the melancholy often remains, a familiar, quiet companion.

Thank you, truly, for spending time with these fragments. For walking alongside me through these unsent words, these late-night reflections, and these lingering feelings. Thank you for witnessing the echoes shared on these pages.

Maybe sharing them like this makes the weight a little less heavy to carry alone. Maybe it keeps the important feelings, the connections – whether real or vividly imagined – alive in a different way, giving them a space to simply *be,* acknowledged and seen.

# Why You Do This To Me

If you'd like to follow along with more
fleeting thoughts, further reflections on
this strange journey we call life, perhaps
more shared words, or future 'maybes', you
can find me continuing the conversation,
sharing fragments as they come, over on
Instagram:

@wordsbyda

Thank you again for reading, for
listening in on the quiet. Take gentle care
of your own heart and its stories.

Maybe... just maybe... we'll meet again
somehow, in words or otherwise.

Maybe.

- da